Get ready! Get ready to experience how poems linking surprise to feeling fire-up your own creative synapses. Prepare yourself to absorb the deep textures of skin and its life-long capacity to remember. These poems possess a crisp, bright, wetness — a delicious sense of Eros. Greensfelder's poems are exactly what one wants and expects when biting the apple, when living a full life.

— **John Fox, author of** *Poetic Medicine: The Healing Art of Poem-Making* **and Founder of The Institute for Poetic Medicine**

This delightful collection spans nearly 70 years of the poet's experience tasting apples in the Garden of her life, beginning with her earliest memories as a child of three and ending with observations about grandchildren. The poems of loss of innocence are often sad, subtly nuanced, and always witty and well crafted. Greensfelder has a gifted eye for the poignant detail, the apt metaphor. As good poetry should, these poems evoke insights about ourselves and the light and dark world of which we are all apple-biting by-products.

— **Margaret Van Every, author of** *A Pillow Stuffed with Diamonds* **(2011) and** *Saying Her Name* **(2012)**

In this coming of age and beyond book, Greensfelder writes with humor and charm. Federico Garcia Lorca said the essence of poetry was in "el vulnerado." Biting the Apple reveals this vulnerability from the child who faces life's pain to the adult who finds survival skills. Biting the Apple is a delightful and moving verse memoir.

— **Glenna Luschei, Past Poet Laureate San Luis Obispo, Editor & Publisher of Solo Press**

D1616404

First edition, December 2012
Copyright © 2012 Jeanie Greensfelder

Published by Penciled In
296 Higuera Street
San Luis Obispo, CA 93401
penciledin.com

ISBN: 1939502004
ISBN-13:   978-1-939502-00-1

Book and Cover Design by Ben Lawless

Cover photos provided by the author

Author's photo by Alexandra Sutton

Penciled In logo design built using icon by
Kevin Sturdevant from The Noun Project

Apple illustration used as section markers designed by
Michell Laurence from The Noun Project

Text is set in Adobe Garamond Pro and Avenir LT Std

BITING THE APPLE

Poems by Jeanie Greensfelder

To Life!
Jeanie Greensfelder

Contents

Acknowledgements

Thank you to the editors of the publications in which these works
or earlier versions of them previously appeared:

Grand: "San Luis Obispo Mission Plaza"
Journal of Poetic Medicine: "Home Alone"
Kaleidoscope: "People Passing"
Orbis: "In Line: Fiftieth High School Reunion"
Porter Gulch Review: "First Love"
Riptide: "What We Knew in 1947"
The Rag: "The Morning Tangle"
Slo Coast Journal: Monthly page, "Genie's Pocket"
Askew: "In Sixth Grade," and "The Puppies"

With deep appreciation to my guides: John Fox,
Margaret Van Every, Glenna Luschei, Diane Stevens,
Diane Halstead, Anne Desmond, Ben Lawless,
Cambria Writers Group, Mary Poulin, Philip Meyer,
Shana Ross, Karen Merriam, Valerie Goldston,
Greg Conroy, and Andy Greensfelder.
Thank you to all friends and poets
for your support. Nothing is done alone.

To my love, Andy

At Three

I hide behind her skirt
and Mother says *she's shy.*
I learn what I am.
And still I search to find
who hid that day.

The Bad Apple

My father buys a bushel of apples—
These will last us through winter—
and I bounce with glee.
Only eat bruised ones, he says.
Always take a bad apple.

A miser with his prized apples,
he checks each one I choose.

One day with no one home
I dare the dark basement
and pick a perfect apple.

Upstairs I cut it crosswise
and eat around the stars.
I do not fall
into Snow White slumber.

When my father comes home,
I smile in innocence
and he smiles back,
unaware of my new friend
the serpent.

Smoky Mountain High

At daybreak in the Smokies
I saw my first fallen cloud. Mother
called it fog, but it looked like heaven
dropped down to look around.

Billowing white beckoned,
if I could reach it before the sun
took heaven back to be
one more cloud in the sky.

What We Knew In 1947

We knew about George Washington,
the axe, the tree: to never tell a lie.
In second grade we didn't know much, but
we knew Bobby's dad never got to third grade;
we knew to stay away from Hank Parker
who had lice; we knew men in cars would honk
and offer rides, but to just keep walking; we knew
to fend for ourselves after school;
we knew kids from the Hebrew Home
had been left there by their parents; we knew
the neighbor man who touched girls
and asked *Does that feel good?* We knew
to run past the domed insane asylum;
we knew Jamie had fits and fell on the floor—
we knew not to look, but we did; we knew
Joey stole candy from Mr. Wolff's store;
we knew Nick Bell got a beating most nights; and
we knew not to tell grownups what we knew.

Seven Years Old, 1947

I can't run:
the soles of my shoes flap.
Mother gives me money and warns,
The shoemaker doesn't speak English.
He'll write the price on paper.
You wait till they are done.

I enter the dim shop
with its musty smells.
As I take my shoes off
and set them on the counter,
a bent man stops hammering.
He looks at them and I look at
the black in the cracks of his fingers.
He writes $1. I nod and sit.

Putting my shoe on a metal foot,
he positions a new sole,
puts a handful of nails in his mouth,
and pushes out one at a time. Tap, tap.

In this fairy tale
I've met an elf or a troll.
When he finishes, I put on my shoes,
hand him a dollar, open the door
and run.

Reflection

Something
satisfying
sobbing
at the mirror,

seeing
someone
feel sorry
for me.

Home Run

From the basement landing
I scan the dark for monsters
and review my route. I dash
from light bulb to light bulb,
my baseball bases.
I pull each chain and seek
safety at each lit stop.
Past piles of Life magazines,
I round the corner of the coal bin,
reach the game dresser,
retrieve Monopoly,
and bolt up the steps,
chased, almost taken out.
I slam and lock the door.
Home safe.

Childhood Lament

(after reading *Captain Marvel* comics)

Shazam!
Shazam!!!
Goddamn.
Why am
I still
who I am?

Elegy to a Sand Pile, 1945

You arrive, a beach, dumped in our yard.
Taller than me, you're smooth and sticky.

My sister takes a hose, wets you down,
and shows me how to finger and fist a tunnel.
Then she runs around, out of sight,
and burrows so her tunnel meets my tunnel.
After tugging on my hand, she lets go.
We peek at each other. The sun comes out,
and I love her and love you. I feel alive.

Pop is building a driveway,
and someday we may even get a car.
My sister goes in, but I stay with you,
and wonder if you miss the ocean.

On Saturday my brother wheelbarrows sand
and Pop stirs you into the cement. When
you're grey and smooth, he pours you.
On all fours, using a long piece of wood,
he sweeps arcs before you set, solid.

I'm sad to see you go, but I like the new you.
We sit out at night like other families,
and the hose shower cools us.

Recently I saw you,
now brown and buckled with age,
still holding sweeping arcs of hope.

At Age Nine

When I close my eyes
I wonder
if the world disappears.
Narcissus in full bloom,
I want everything
to be about me.

I shut my eyes and try
to make Anastasia disappear:
Anastasia who sucks on my Popsicle,
who puts an arm lock on my neck,
who pulls me around,
who calls me *fruit.*

The Puppies

Perhaps I dreamed our dog had puppies.

Downstairs, lights dim, a woman, my mother,
sits on a stool, her hands submerged in a bucket.
A flick of her head scares me, sends me upstairs,
not to see what I should not see,
not to know what I should not know,
for this dark place is not my place.

Perhaps I dreamed our dog had puppies.

Cemetery Sunday, 1948

Mother filled mayonnaise jars with her iris
and Pop propped them in our '38 Ford.
Still in my jeans, I got yanked away
from playing baseball to go to the Coulterville Cemetery
where we'd meet my aunt and uncle and their daughter.
I got the annual lecture to be nice to my cousin June
who had had polio and how impolite it is
to stare at someone's problems, like June's limp.

Wearing a blue velvet dress, June got out
of their shiny sedan. She was gushy sweet,
and I did my urchin best to act nice
and talk about going into third grade
while we walked, trying not to step on graves.
I hated her for being happy, for ruining my day,
for wanting to come to the Coulterville Cemetery,
for wanting to come with her parents.

My mother placed her iris on the gravesite
and my aunt placed a store-bought vase of gladiolas.
I wondered if my grandparents lying below us
were glad for the company and the flowers,
how they felt, alone in the Coulterville Cemetery,
if they were sorry I missed a baseball game…

I saw my aunt looking at me.
She was staring.

Gone Fishing

Now that we had a car,
Pop bought bamboo poles and bait,
drove us to Creve Coeur Lake
where he and Mother sat in chairs
holding poles, watching buoys,
hoping for bobs.

I didn't know how to swim,
but I stood in the murky water,
moved my arms and pretended.

My father beamed. My mother
smiled at him and smiled at me.
Holding those long magic wands
could take someone anywhere:
they were launched,
faces soft and faraway.

Knitting

There's a thread you follow.

"The Way It Is" William Stafford

I hold out my arms. Mother
puts coils of yarn around them.
Starting with a thread,
she winds ball after ball,
colors for her afghan.

I did not know then
that life holds out its arms
and starting with a thread,
I knit my story.

Easter Duty

Wearing chagrin and last year's dress,
I slink into the Christian Science
Sunday School. Mother makes
me go on holidays.

Pious regulars remember me,
know my parents don't come,
know I don't read the weekly lesson,
know I don't report healings,
and know that I don't know the Truth.

While the teacher talks, I look up
at Mary Baker Eddy's pastel portrait,
an old woman with a high lace collar,
short hair in gray waves,
kind of a smiling George Washington.

Staring at the words *God is Love*,
I imagine getting out of here,
out of this taffeta dress, into my jeans,
back to biking in the streets.

Sixth Grade

We didn't like each other,
but Lynn's mother had died,
and my father had died.

Lynn's father didn't know how to talk to her,
my mother didn't know how to talk to me,
and Lynn and I didn't know how to talk either.

A secret game drew us close:
we took turns being the prisoner,
who stood, hands held behind her back,

while the captor, using an imaginary bow,
shot arrow after arrow after arrow
into the prisoner's heart.

Twelve Years Old, 1952

Mary Anne sports braces on her buckteeth
like she owns a new Cadillac and they
cost as much. She flips a rubber band at me
and invites me into her dark and musty house.

In her room we shut the door
and flop on her bed.
We hear a stern voice downstairs
and Mary Anne whispers,
My sister got home last night.
She went away to have a baby.
A boy. She gave him away.

She tumbles on top of me, and says
Is this what they do? Lifting my sweater,
she rubs my buds: *Have to massage them,*
you know. She turns over and offers hers:
We have to practice, but not get in trouble.
Mom says my sister's labeled for life.

Hungry, we go to the kitchen.
Mary Anne's sister sits at the table.
Next to her, their mother stands,
staring up and praying aloud,
Mary, Mary, forgive my daughter's sins.
My friend hands me an apple and I bite into it.

First Love

My first boyfriend was my second choice:
Beth got Gerry Jenson so I got Billy James
whose jaw hung, his tongue showing.

I looked down on Billy: girls were taller
in seventh grade. I wore his ID bracelet
and a motorcycle cap with his initials.

When we hugged, he smelled like Ivory soap,
his cheek smooth and soft—a Norman Rockwell boy.
Walking me home from school he carried my books,

and looked forward to a kiss at my door.
I knew he was trustworthy and true,
reliably mine, but Billy didn't know me:

I'd met a tall guy who drove a Ford.
His cheeks were sandpaper rough
and he French kissed.

And on this day on my front porch,
when Billy handed me my books,
I handed him his ID bracelet

and watched his face redden, his eyes tear,
hurt bursting his seams. We both cried
soap-opera style, and Billy ran home.

In my room, I draped myself over my bed,
like an actress far away from home,
pained and in love with drama.

So Much To See, 1957

I followed him up three flights of stairs.
An inventor, he pressed three buttons by his door
made it buzz ajar, and said *Open Sesame.*
Come in to my world.

I saw orange canvas butterfly chairs,
cushions on a low foam pad,
and a matted jute rug.
Bookcases stood along burlap walls
and egg crates covered the ceiling.
I stared at a self-portrait of his wife,
an artist with a black braid on one shoulder.
Twenty years of trouble, he said. *She's leaving.*

He steered me into his darkroom,
where he shined magic yellow lights
and turned paper into photographs.

In his shop he assembled parts
and made an ugly lamp for my college dorm.

I saw so much when I was there,
but failed to see this was
my future home.

Breaking Up, 1957

She stood in the wood and glass phone booth,
dialed the operator, deposited coins,
and watched classmates walk across campus
for breakfast. Shaking, she waited, then said,
We need to break up. I called to say goodbye.

He would not listen: she had turned eighteen,
he had gotten his divorce, he was driving up,
they'd elope today, she'd be his wife.

She hung up, slumped down
and sat on her heels in the booth.
She'd failed to say goodbye.

Now, a star in a drama,
she was about to cause havoc.

Wanting her family to suffer,
she used to imagine her funeral.
Now she'd get to watch.

Going Out

At a gala picnic before the opera,
the lawn is dotted with white tables
and people tuxedoed and gowned.
Couples mingle and chat in this
throwback to prom night.

A friend of my ex, a French designer
who had us over for prime rib
and Yorkshire pudding, stares at me.
I'm sure she's remembering my turn to cook:
pot roast and smashed potatoes.

I dodge a nice, but boring, couple,
see a woman wave, then turn away,
and I realize she's avoiding me.

I hate this dressing up and going out
yet long to be accepted
in the land of pretense:
prince and Cinderella balls.
For me it's midnight
and I'm found out.

I go inside to my seat,
safe, until my daughter's
nursery-school teacher smiles
and my failings as a mother flash.

The hardest part of going out
is running into myself.

Visit To My New Husband's Office, 1974

I gaze at the glass skyscraper, inhale,
push the revolving door, and take the elevator
to the thirty-third floor law offices.
Through the ten-foot tall door,
I find my new husband, who opens his arms.

I see his cherry-wood desk and credenza,
comfy client chairs, a Klee print,
a ficus tree. Floor to ceiling windows
overlook the courthouse dome, the Arch,
and a towboat pushing coal-filled barges.

Though I knew what to expect, I'm shaken.
Seeing him there—Brooks Brothers blue,
Johnson-Murphy feet—he's a stranger,
more important than I. I can't breathe.

Unaware of my dismay, he keeps talking:
Can't open the darn windows. No air.
Yes, I say. *No air at all.*

Stop The World

I agree with the man who wrote
Stop the World—I Want to Get Off
because people aren't kind and good,
because I have to be perfect and I fail,
because I have to suffer and repent,
because I join my husband on his business trip,
because that puts me in downtown Los Angeles,
because the sun shines bright and I want to hide,
because everyone sees I don't belong,
because briefcasers rush in all directions,
because my mind judges my every move,
because the museum cashier stares at me,
because at the outdoor escalator a black man sings,
because he talks straight up to people,
because he says, *Where all you people goin'?*
because he clearly belongs in this world,
because I'm lost with no breadcrumb trail,
because I find my hotel and rush to my room,
because I sigh relief when I close the door,
because I climb under the covers and cry,
because I fall asleep and for awhile
I stop the world and get off.

Looking Back

Shoot me into outer space,
that place where light from 1939
arrives just now, and I can see into St. Louis,
into Deaconess Hospital, watch my birth,
and find out if a nurse held me tight.
I hear my mother lament one more baby
with her husband fired, sister taking her in,
and kids farmed out to relatives.

Let me follow my father to his brother's
where he shoots a gun into the ceiling.
Show me Danville Veterans' Hospital
where they shelve my father
and give him shock treatments.

He's shaking on a table. I can't look.

Send me to when he comes home.
I'm two. We play piggyback and blocks,
both of us children.

The Homestead

...a farm that is no more a farm.

"Directive" — Robert Frost

Growing up on a Kentucky farm,
she fed the pigs and chickens,
picked beans and strawberries,
lugged water from the well,
carried wood for weekly baths,
shivered in the cold outhouse,
and when she was old enough,
she left and never looked back,

except that one trip, cross-country,
when she tried to find
the town that was no more a town,
the farm that was no more a farm,
and stood there in a field looking
like she'd lost the Grail goblet,
and wanted to sip once more,
to find the sweet in the bitter.

A Champs-Élysées Stroll, 1980

On a torrid day, traffic and tourists sweat
and we trudge toward Café Laureé.
I'm determined to taste the famed macaroons
my friend raved about.

My husband sights a nearby brasserie
and wants to skip the Café Laureé,
souring my Paris magic.
I hurl vintage hurts at him:
You don't love me. You never loved me.
His eyes flare and his lips quiver.

Then his body snakes across ten lanes of cars,
leaving me gilded in guilt, scared and stranded,
staring at the Arch of Triumph.
He had stopped smoking,
and returns, puffing a cigarette,
punishing me, hurting himself.

Two tired tourists call a truce.
We march in league down the *Champs*
toting a memory, a slice of time
toasted with heat, hot words, and smoke.

Me and My Shadow

Sun low in the sky,
I walk my shadow, watch
the long black of me
stretch tall across the road.

A car drives past
and my shadow lifts,
flows over hood, roof, and trunk
to lie back down on the pavement.

Ah, to have my shadow's skill
not to get run over by life—
to flow over obstacles
and keep on walking.

Interlude

Esalen's hot tubs perch on a cliff
over the Pacific. Steamy sulfur rises,
lures me down the hill.

Several bare bodies share a stone basin,
and a man suns on a massage table.

Swimsuits violate mores here.
Down steps, past a fountain,
I enter a room with benches and hooks,
and hang inhibitions with my clothes.

As bodies pass,
many flawed and few flawless,
the unusual becomes the usual.
The tubs look out on surf
smashing rocks below.
I watch for otters and let the
hot water soothe me.

Warmed inside and out I dress,
gather my inhibitions
and walk up the hill.

Prius Phone Booth

Behind the wheel of a car
some people remain themselves,
but in my Prius phone booth
I forgo my meek and mild persona

and turn superhero bold,
a don't-mess-with-me driver.

My Prius and I troll streets,
face off at stop signs with SUVs and Lexi,
swivel for U-turns, and
parallel park with panache.

Back in the walking world,
shy and ready to defer, I keep
a firm grasp on my smart key.

Daring Danger

A crowd watches
twenty-foot waves crash
on the jetty behind Morro Rock.
Ocean swells explode
invoking dread and desire.

Controlled danger
compelled me to come.
I practice fear, then relief,
not like my burst appendix,
not like my brother dropping dead,
not like life crashing in on me.

Lizzie, My Lizard

The brain's amygdala,
nicknamed lizard-brain,
stays ever alert and wary.

Honed on fear and survival,
my Lizzie pumps cortisol
and disables my cerebral cortex.

Give her a symptom and
Lizzie stalks it to my demise:
sniffles become pneumonia;
a mole becomes melanoma.

Unsure of my acuity, she
repeats her report,
repeats her report,
repeats her report.

Desperate to silence her
I picture holding Lizzie,
stroking her scaly skin,
then containing her in a
terrarium. Through glass,
we stare at each other.

I study this creature
primed to keep me alive
even if it kills me.

People Passing

By the grocery, a homeless man smokes.
Seeing me, he hides his cigarette,
stands up, nods his head, and says,
Ma'am, may you have a beautiful day.
His greeting follows me into the store
where I gather green beans and bread.
On leaving, I plan to thank the man,
and talk to him, but he's gone.

The neighborhood yardman unloads
his truck and emotions—he had
another fight with his son,
he just can't stop.

Later, near the beach--a gull eyes
my smoked-salmon taco, and
a boy whizzes by in his wheelchair.
I say *Great day!* to a woman passing—
she frowns and shrugs her shoulders.

On my evening walk, a man
parks his clunky red Thunderbird,
gets out, sets his puppy on the roof,
and reaches inside for packages. I say,
Cute dog, cute car, and pass by. Behind me, I hear
Ma'am! Ma'am! Cute car, cute dog…what about me?
I look back and smile at the disheveled man.

In bed I remember Browning's poem,
"Pippa Passes," about a little girl walking,
unaware of the effect she has on townspeople.
Thinking of the Pippas I passed today,
I wonder if one of them
lies in bed thinking of me.

The Morning Tangle

I walk and meditate, and I'm famished.
My husband returns from swimming laps.
With unplanned synchronicity
we take our places in the kitchen.
He hoards the cutting board,
slices a peach and banana.
I prepare coffee. We pivot for a
choreographed collision at the refrigerator,
him for almond milk, me for an egg and jam.

We exchange no words, for
we are dangerous before we eat.

With our preparations complete,
I covet his bowl of cereal and fruit,
and he eyes my lightly-over egg and toast.

Safely seated in a no-chatter zone,
we take favored newspaper sections.
Earlier I meditated on wherever I go, there I am.
My mantra shifts: wherever I go, there he is.

Hypnos, God of Sleep

He creeps into my bed,
envelops me,
erases my worries,
and together
we dream.

But on those nights
when he doesn't show,
and I know he's out
sleeping with others,
I wait and watch and
add him to my worries.

He ruins my nights,
disturbs my days,
and he never listens.

My counselor says,
You're stuck with him.
Calm him with chamomile,
soothe him with love talk.

That night he watches
as I brew his tea,
bathe, dab lavender,
turn on Brahms,
and get into bed early,
hoping he's pleased,
hoping he stays the night.

Home Alone

He ghosts about the house,
reminding me to take out the trash,
to push the can for pickup,
to find the paper in the bushes,
and to start coffee.

He'd do it, but he's gone on retreat.
We each practice losing the other.
He's stronger, can cope with more,
but odds favor me to be the one
to face loneliness, figure finances,
and master the thermostat.

I try to twist open a jar of jelly.
He watches and wishes me well.

The Drought Ends

The baptismal first rain
makes me sing and skip—
I'm in a Gene Kelly movie.

My umbrella protects me
and I spin the stem making spray.
Pings turn steady and strong,
the street becomes a stream,
and my socks are soaked.

My mind flits to the film
Life with Father when, at nine,
I learned the requirement
for heaven: baptism.
I ran home to say,
I need to be baptized!

How my mom laughed:
*You want some minister
to come throw water in your face?*

Suddenly, now, I fling my umbrella,
face the sky, and answer her,

Yes. Yes. Yes.

The Staging

Imagine a clear complexion, the doctor says,
My laser could fix that red spot.

My mind flashes to my deathbed:
Too tired to dab makeup and
about to leave a lasting impression,
which do I want to hear—
Too bad about that red spot   or
My, such beautiful skin?

Those real-estate folks who showcase homes
create illusions to please buyers
could stage my departure.
They might place a flower in my hair,
a humble daisy or go wild with an orchid,
matched with a floral gown and then
add flowered wallpaper as well.
The house overlooks the ocean,
the sun streams in just so,
and at night, moonlight.
A cello concerto begins.

No eyes open, no mouth gaping—
cached above me, pink rose petals
float down to contrast
with the red rose over my heart.
Realtors, they think of everything!

A film crew captures my final exit,
sends it to You Tube,
and people around the world
admire my complexion.

Heart

I walk my dream dog—
Heart needs no leash.
She bounds ahead, then runs back,
herds me to see what she sees:
a blooming bird of paradise.

A barometer,
she jumps into my arms,
looks me over to see
if I need attention.
Then she's back to sniffing life.

Heart came to me in a dream
and stayed.

In Line: Fiftieth High School Reunion

As teen-aged seniors
we cheer our Pirates
until skull and crossbones fly.

Fifty years flash by.
Now we are the grown-ups
we once laughed at

and need old yearbooks
to know who's who
and ask, *What's new?*

We remember those who died:
    Stevie wrote our *Buccaneer* song
    Larry promised the girls his love
    Joan teased the new kids
    Sandy wore cashmere every day
    Parker captained our Pirates team

We queue behind them now,
walking the plank,

but
we
don't
know
our
place
in
line.

Sparrows and Hawk

I wish we didn't have to die...
she's four, sitting in her yard,

picking dandelion puffs
and blowing seeds.

Her new baby brother cries.
I hold and soothe him.

She looks at him and smiles:
He's too cute to kill.

My niece surprises me with what
she knows and doesn't know.

Life is served with death.
Do we know this or learn this?

My wish echoes hers. Above
a red-tailed hawk hunts.

Sparrows voice alarm,
hide in the thicket.

My Seduction

The book *Botany of Desire**
reveals that plants use wiles
to entice people to promote
their proliferation.

Apples and potatoes
tempt with taste,
tulips with beauty, and
marijuana with intoxication.

Now, my garden lures me
like Amsterdam's red light district:
lilies and lavender hawk their wares.
Grape vine tendrils reach for me.
Jasmine dares me to sniff
and swoon, invites me
to be a love-slave,
and I say,

Yes. Yes. Take me.

*by Michael Pollan

Thoughts on Thoughts

One cold day, drying myself after a shower,
I notice my husband's towel hung over a heating vent.
If anything ever happens to him, I think,
I'll get the warm towel bar.

When I tell him my thought, he laughs and says,
I haven't pictured your demise since yesterday
when you ate the last chocolate.

What's It Like To Be Old?

Don't get me started! Why do you ask?
Am I defensive? Yes. Of course I want
to slide back, get a re-ride, slip into that
summer skin I failed to appreciate.

I'm still that girl, but no one knows and
I'm stuck at restaurants with birds of my feather,
a misfit, flocked with a covey of old folks
while I imagine being with the youth nearby.

I didn't join; I got drafted—hurled into
wrinkled wisdom, unscrewed, even screwy
with perspective and perception. Deliver me
from red hats and wearing purple. See me shop
the Banana Republic to flirt with dudes.

I'm not so old I don't remember teenage pain:
being turned inside out by what others thought.
A pawn of my id, I craved attention and spent
those years in a playground of despair,
hope and disaster, love and loss.

As a teen, I saw thirty as curtains
and sixty as suicide time.
Do you really want to know what it's like?
Well, so do I. I'm still learning at seventy.
Ninety is the new old age. I'm in my prime.

We

The sun sears hot this morning,
comes down hard.

At breakfast, we stop to laugh.
He laughs when I say
we need to do something
when I mean *he needs* to. I just said
we need to get the ladder to change a light bulb.

We laugh extra as we age,
look at each other a second too long,
see our inner roulette wheels spin,
and know the one left standing
will remember this moment.

The sun sears hot this morning,
comes down hard.

Babe

In grade school Betty called me *Babe*.
Our club pasted cartoons in a book
and took it to Children's Hospital.
We bobbed for apples, danced the two-step,
and played spin the bottle with boys.

Betty never went to high school
yet kept in touch with classmates.
She knew the growing families,
and planned Canasta nights.
I found excuses and didn't go.

Moving on, I never looked back.
Years later at a supermarket, Betty saw me
and called out, *Babe! How are you, Babe?*
Hoping no one heard her, I stiffened
and said, politely, *Fine, thank you, Betty.*

Suddenly, at seventy, I call Betty
who tells me Carolyn has Alzheimer's,
Delores died years ago,
and Billy had to retire as a fireman,
but gets to drive the fire truck in parades.

I'm doin' okay, Betty says, *that darn diabetes—
no more lemon meringue pie.*

Sad now that I turned my back on her,
turned my back on my self,
I can't wait to hear her say,
So glad you called, Babe.

San Luis Obispo Mission Plaza

She pulls me along the red tile stripes
that crisscross the plaza—*Don't touch
the cement Grandma*—and she giggles.
She's in charge and I'm her charge,
willing to follow her anywhere
to taste her three-year-old joy.

Etching this moment in my mind,
seeing her as happy as happy can be,
I know she won't remember it as she
moves on to school, braces and boys.
If she's lucky one day
she will mother and grandmother

and be pulled back to this place.

To The New Year

You burst from the starting gate
and though I pull on the reins,
I hang on for the ride,
longing for 1940's snail-pace years
when I wanted to be older, faster, sooner.

Now you race through weeks and months,
rushing to your demise. Do you ever
think of jumping fence,
lying in green pasture,
letting me slip from the saddle
to the spacious terrain of silence
where I can breathe
reflections about my life,
feel the texture of grass,
and gaze into your tender eyes?

Sailing

From the deck of a cruise ship
leaving San Francisco, I gaze
at the Golden Gate Bridge, and try not
to imagine those who have jumped.

Wind pushes against me,
lets me know I'm going somewhere—
I wish I were wild, hopping a freighter
for the south seas and beyond.

While I long to be a pilot or a diver,
a climber or a surfer, or even a bartender
meeting and tending to travelers,
I'm grateful as I recall my journey:

What are you thankful for? a teacher asked.
Bubble gum and ice cream, I said.
I never knew I loved parents who called me in
when I wanted to play hide and seek till dawn.

At school I played jacks on the lunch table,
pig in a basket, putting pieces in my palm.
I never knew I loved the cafeteria line,
having hair-netted women fill my plate.

I never knew I loved bumblebees. Could one
love a bumblebee, the one that sat on
my belt buckle when I was alone in the yard
trying to be a statue, staring into its eyes?

I'm beyond feeling I didn't belong in those
teen years when the world didn't want me, and
left me in tears. Now, under the Golden Gate,
I feel for those who chose the bridge.

On this voyage, breathing sweet salt air,
I run with a butterfly net
catching and cataloging moments,
risking loving life to death.

At Seventy

Decades cross like comets,
years fall like shuffled cards:
now you see them, now you don't.

Memories live on:
finding my ribs in the mirror;
pounding the sofa to make dust germs rise;
praying at age eight to wake up twenty-four;
going to see my father in a coma;
planning to die at sixty and never grow old;
leading Pep Club meetings in tears;
eloping from college at eighteen;
beaming at my daughter's third Christmas;
waking at twenty-four, wanting to be eight;
hearing the rabbi bless my second marriage;
communing with a Luna moth in our A-frame.

I hold the core of my apple
and nibble slowly.

About the Author

Jeanie Greensfelder grew up in St. Louis, Missouri. A psychologist, she seeks to understand herself and others on this shared journey, filled, as Joseph Campbell wrote, with sorrowful joys and joyful sorrows. Now living on the central coast of California with her husband Andy, she writes poetry.

Her poems have been published in *Askew, Echoes, Grand, Orbis, Kaleidoscope, Porter Gulch Review, Journal of Poetic Medicine, Riptide, The Rag,* and *Yellow Bricks and Ruby Slippers.* "Genie's Pocket" can be seen monthly at *slocoastjournal.com.*